ADORE YOUR DREAMS

(AN ANTHOLOGY OF POEMS)
(PAPERBACK, DECEMBER 2024)

COMPILED & EDITED BY
DR. SONIA GUPTA

DEDICATED TO

DREAM IT
THEN
make it
HAPPEN

CONTENTS

FOREWORD

"An amazing anthology motivating us to believe in our goals and dreams."

A person chooses goals in his life to lead him forward for self-realization. Thus, his days are filled with meaning and the pursuit of happiness. Wise people use their time in life to succeed. "Dreams are the seeds of change." - says Debby Boone. Yesterday has passed, leaving us with memories. Tomorrow will be different; today's desires can come true in it. Dreamers offer bold and unexpected solutions. Their discoveries transform reality and humanity moves forward.

*Dr. Sonia Gupta offers a new anthology **"ADORE YOUR DREAMS"** that collects poems of various dream trajectories: unfulfilled, every day, endless, joyous, mysterious, heavenly. Authors ask where the overwhelming desire and pursuit of happiness comes from, then where it disappears. Sometimes longing reaches heavenly heights, and holds all nature with the sun, moon and clouds. Sometimes life feels like hell, but with dreams in your eyes and heart and a strong belief that they will come true someday, the dark night brightens. The success comes slowly, sometimes painfully, but dreamers continue on their way. The poets remind us not to forget that each of us is indispensable to all creatures. They advise us not to blame ourselves, and not to feel like victims on difficult days. Spring comes after winter. Let's wait patiently. Dreams create the future. Actions are needed to make them come true. To believe in the chosen goals and to continue on our way to their realization. In the coming days, the seeds of our imaginations germinate, grow and blossom.*

Anthology after anthology, Dr. Sonia Gupta has compiled, edited and published dozens of thematic collections for which I had the honour of writing forewords or reviews. In them, she included poets from all over the world, and enriched the literature of humanity with new voices and unexpected perspectives on life and its values. Her monthly published literary e-magazine, 'Canvas of Thoughts', each issue of which is dedicated to a different theme, has gained wide popularity. The present volume **"ADORE YOUR DREAMS"** *is another beautiful bird that flies to the readers. Today again it is my pleasure to write the foreword for her new anthology. Through the words of the authors, their strong and true maxims, pictures and advice, the book adds beauty, optimism, knowledge and poetic sublimity to our lives. It dispels dark thoughts, makes us dream of happy moments and strengthens our faith in the power and success of good. Amazing are the compositions of budding young poets. My special wishes to these little gems. Admirations to Dr. Sonia Gupta for her tireless efforts to take the art of poetry to greater heights. Our congratulations and gratitude to the literary devotee Dr. Sonia Gupta as well as to the talent and positivity of the poets included in this remarkable anthology.*

Stoianka Boianova
(Poet, Reviewer & Critic)
Sofia, Bulgaria

Whispers of Leaves

I write letters on cherry petals -
A wind carries them
I recreate verses in my mind
Whirlwinds lift them up to the sky-high
To the astral
With the whisper of the leaves.

We are in the chorus of art!
We feel the whole world as a homeland
We have lived in the times.
Our dream is to be brothers with people,
With the animals - friends
And may harmony flourish on Earth!

© Stoianka Boianova

About the Reviewer

She is a poet, writer, author, editor and reviewer. She has authored eleven books: poetry, novel and short stories. and co-authored four bilingual books, poetry and haiku – in India with Minko Tanev. She has participated in over 60 international anthologies and publications with numerous awards and recognitions. She edits dictionaries and books. She is in the European Top 100 of the most creative haiku authors. She won several awards, "First World Poetry Competition of Newspapers and Televisions", 2020, China, Chinese International Zhengxin Poet Award, 2022, International Poetry Prize "Ossi di Seppia", 2023, Italy. She is a Chairwoman of Haiku Club – Plovdiv, an editorial board member of "Haiku Sviat/Haiku World" magazine. She is also a member of PEN Bulgaria, Union of the Bulgarian Writers, the Bulgarian haiku Union, the Haiku Foundation – USA, United Haiku and Tanka Society – UK, the World Haiku Association, Japan, Global Honorary Council of Federation of World Culture & Art Society (Singapore). She is a Physicist and has worked in the field of measurement accuracy - metrology, standardization, certification, authorization.

- *Facebook ID:*
  https://www.facebook.com/stoianka.boianova.3
- ***Email ID****: stboianova@abv.bg*

PREVIEW-1

"A beautiful compilation that inspires us to value our dreams"

*In the selected works from another poetry anthology, **"ADORE YOUR DREAMS"** compiled & edited by Dr. Sonia Gupta, we learn to live and adore our dreams. According to poets, even if life takes us down the thorniest paths, we are sure that one-day dreams will come true. Their magic wand mystery transforms history.*

What else is left for us but to swear: never to give in and give up on our dreams. For those who face tyranny - we have ambitions in our eyes to make them come true and we are sure to achieve them. Deep, in the depths of our hearts, we carry the purest longing for freedom against the fear of death and slavery, we follow the impulse of aspirations embodied in verses that no one or nothing can erase.

From the negatives, positives peek out, if we breathe new life into them. Shadows seem to disappear from the visions. We are filled with desires before the cherished questions: where we came from and where we are going. Dreams live in us. Longings for flight, for life. In them, we look for open skies and every glance finds the direction. To smile at ourselves, making sense of seemingly impossible things. The world will be a more beautiful place where all creatures coexist and abound in their natural diversity. We are filled with joy and bliss in the eternal game of life. These are lights in our souls and colorful worlds with galaxies immeasurable.

*Dr. Sonia Gupta is an established poet and author of twenty-eight independent books, editor of several anthologies, poems and magazines, translator and reviewer. I feel glad to be a part of her projects. Presenting anthologies on meaningful and important themes, she is doing a remarkable job in the field of literature that will be admired forever. Today, again it's my pleasure to scribble my words for her new anthology, **"ADORE YOUR DREAMS"**. We are grateful to Dr. Sonia Gupta and the poets for inspiring optimism. Indeed it is a beautiful compilation that inspires us to value our dreams and to keep their flicker illuminated, enlightening our soul and heart to cherish the reality of these dreams in our lives forever. One of the amazing aspects of this anthology is the poems composed by young budding poets. My special wishes to these little gems. My congratulations to Dr. Sonia Gupta and all the poets for their determined spirit to create this new anthology.*

- Minko Tanev
(Poet, Reviewer & Critic)
Sofia, Bulgaria

Chorale

Awesome galactic emotions
Turned our dreams into dust -
In the hearts of whirlwinds I survived
In the poems of stellar bards.

Supreme leaders and super-personalities
Find the clear destiny path –
Their own sacred power to embody -
Cosmic rhythm is in everything.

In metamorphoses impenetrable
Poetry immortalized them
And with the rumble of the heavy doors
We to enter the temple and let us repent.

© Minko Tanev

About the Reviewer

He is a poet, writer, author, editor and reviewer. He has authored 6 books and co-authored 4 bilingual books, poetry and haiku – in India with Stoianka Boianova. He has participated in over 60 International anthologies and publications with numerous awards and recognitions. He has edited over 70 books. He is in the European Top 100 of the most creative haiku authors. He has won several awards, "First World Poetry Competition of Newspapers and Televisions", 2020, China, Chinese International Zhengxin Poet Award, 2022, International Poetry Prize "Ossi di Seppia", 2023, Italy. He is a member of Union of the Bulgarian Writers, the Bulgarian haiku Union, the Haiku Foundation – USA, United Haiku and Tanka Society – UK, the World Haiku Association, Japan, Global Honorary Council of Federation of World Culture & Art Society (Singapore). He is a Philologist - Bulgarian language. He was a lecturer of Bulgarian language for foreign students – Medical University, Plovdiv.

Facebook ID: *https://www.facebook.com/minko.tanev.9*
Email ID: *minkotanev@abv.bv*

PREVIEW-2

"The biggest adventure you can ever take is to live the life of your dreams".

- Oprah Winfrey

Dreams can be defined in multiple ways, including a series of thoughts, pictures, or feelings that occur during sleep, or a goal that is longed for. It's a wonderful thing you can create in your imagination, most often related to your future. Something you hope and wish to achieve someday. Dreaming is a very deep and profound thinking process in which we focus solely on the self. Through dreaming, we examine our current issues, behaviours and goals. Whilst our slumberous dreams are vital and fundamental to our physical and mental well-being it is also applicable in our waking life too. We all as humans have deep-embedded dreams, ambitions and aspirations of many kinds. What matters is that we should use them as a focal point in our lives, to move forward, growing and evolving. Becoming a better person in the process as we move forward, get closer to achieving those dreams and make new ones in the process.

*Taking "Dreams" as the central theme of this anthology Dr. Sonia Gupta has again come up with a new collection of endearing poems **"ADORE YOUR DREAMS"**. The anthology consists of fifty poets from around the world, each of whom has penned beautiful and unique poems about dreams and what they mean and represent to them. Each one is wonderfully expressive in its words, imagery and passion. Amazing are these dreamers, these artists, these creative souls that stretch the imaginations' very boundaries.*

*Dr. Sonia Gupta has already edited numerous anthologies and write-ups of different poets and authors throughout the world. This current anthology **"ADORE YOUR DREAMS"**. is yet another achievement for her as an Editor. A renowned author of 28 independently published books in English and Hindi, she is making her mark on the pages of literature with her contributions. I am very honoured to be a part of her projects, for which I wrote previews. This for me has been and will continue to be very memorable. I am truly amazed by the way she accomplishes her tasks before the given time. Presenting different poets from different regions on a single platform and providing them with the opportunity to contribute to literature altogether is an appreciable effort made by her. I congratulate her on another marvellous anthology that is full of beautiful dreamy ink that lifts, inspires and makes you think about the bigger things in life. I am sure this book will be well received and will inspire, resonate and uplift its readers. May everyone's dreams come true, dream BIG my friends!!*

-Donna McCabe
(Poet & Reviewer)
Rhondda, South Wales, UK.

Dreams Come True

Sail away on the sea of hope,
Bound for the land of love,
Walk through the valley of dreams come true,
Whispered magic of earthly powers.

Harmony floats upon the breeze,
Fingers of twilight caress the land
Like treasures of wisdom evading my touch,
The fading light, a velvet blue sky.

Carry me away into the night,
Search the sky for moonbeams,
Touch the sea of tenderness,
Place the silver moon in my hands.

Touch my heart and my soul,
Touch the thoughts of my mind,
Touch my life and you will find,
The castle of everlasting love.

© Donna McCabe

About the Reviewer

She is an established poet with over 20 years of experience whose vast variety of work has gained her multiple accolades within her field of literature over the years. From being published in journals, magazines and anthologies as well as being a highly respected admin in multiple social media groups, she is a regular contributor to literature. Besides this, she is an artist also. Her intricate wordplay displayed in her works has been personified by her past and concurrent experiences which include her hardships, trials and tribulations. Her lifetime admiration of reading and writing and love of art has steered her into an adventurous new direction of collaborations with an up-and-coming Canadian artist Ala Ilescu whose idiosyncratic mind and artistic works compliment the vivid images her narrative works paint. These collaborations have resulted in a beautiful book of poetry and artwork entitled "Explosion of Love" published on Amazon. Her creativity has also taken her onto other platforms in recent times, Using Instagram to reach out and display her love of writing, artwork, and love of the natural world to a wider audience. Her writings and interactions with the wider poetry communities there have helped her gain a good following and many features and awards.

- ***Email id-*** *donna_salisbury@sky.com*
- ***Instagram page*** *-@donnamccabe_*
- ***Facebook page-*** *Poemsbydonnamcc*

PREFACE

*Poetry has been known to be the simplest way to express our feelings for the ages. A poet paints a wonderful canvas on blank paper with the ink of imagination and feelings flowing freely without any binding or fear. We have published several anthologies on different themes to date. Continuing that journey, a thought came into my mind to bring a new anthology dedicated to DREAMS. Our lives revolve around our DREAMS; every one of us knows this. DREAMS are not only imaginations but our guide and inspiration too. They ignite the spark of inner motivation and encourage us to move further on life's pathway to achieve our goals and ambitions. Every one of us sees DREAMS but not all dare to turn them into reality. For many, DREAMS are merely an entertainment source. But the ones who understand their values, put their efforts into making these DREAMS true and they keep alive them always until they are fulfilled. This is the cantered theme of the current anthology in your hands **"ADORE YOUR DREAMS"**. Through these poems, poets have expressed different thoughts about DREAMS. But one single message that is being gained by these verses is that DREAMS are our pathfinders and guides, motivating us to turn the impossible into possible. We must live our DREAMS & adore them always. And taking this message, I was motivated to keep the title of the book **"ADORE YOUR DREAMS"**. All verses are full of optimism, hope and new wishes. The poems are simple, sublime, melodious and tender, touching the hearts of readers. Contributions by many budding young poets have added more beauty to this anthology. These poetic souls are for other poets and writers.*

As an Editor, I had a huge responsibility on my shoulders to select the poems, compile, edit and design this anthology. I have tried my best to accomplish my job. Here, one thing I would like to highlight is that the role of editing regarding punctuation, commas, capitalization of the first letter, etc. is excluded from my side because different poets had their own assumptions and not everyone was happy to follow a common rule. So, the poems have been placed as per the choice of the poets. For any plagiarism, the editor is not responsible, poets have submitted their poems along with a declaration. The entire anthology has been designed by me, including the cover page. The picture on the cover page has been taken from internet resources. Though I am an artist and wanted to paint it myself, owing to some health issues, it was not possible this time. I appreciate the timeless contribution, dedication, and cooperation shown by the poets from day one until the end of this project. I am sure after reading these verses, everyone will start believing in their own potential and feel the magic of this simple virtue that leads to crossing all odds and hurdles coming on life's pathway. I congratulate my entire team, including the poets and reviewers for their wonderful contributions. Let us keep alive the flicker of our DREAMS and adore our DREAMS forever.

- Dr. Sonia Gupta
(Editor)

ACKNOWLEDGEMENTS

I usually hear these words: "If we say Thank You to someone, it means we are bowing our heads in front of that Lord only". We can forget anything in life, but we should never forget to Thank someone who has helped or motivated us in any way. I am a medical professional and I never thought that one day I would become a writer, poet and author. It is all a miracle and a dream for me. But now it has become my passion, my inspiration and an integral part of my life. It's all by God's grace that he honoured me with such a unique gift. And the amazing aspect of this achievement is that everything I have gained during the odd and dark phase of my life. To accomplish any task, there are many invisible hands behind which shower abundant blessings, motivating us to achieve our destination. In the same way, in completing this book, I have been blessed and encouraged by so many for whom I am GRATEFUL by my heart.

First of all, I thank the Goddess of knowledge and wisdom, Maa Saraswati, who gave me the strength to complete this work and encouraged me to pick up my pen to compile, edit and prepare this anthology. In the world, everything changes, but one thing that never changes is our parents. Heartfelt thanks to my parents for their faith in me and showering their infinite blessings on me. Special thanks to my father, who has left this materialistic world to attain the embrace of the divine Lord. He had been my inspiration and will be forever, and his teachings illuminate my life's pathway like an enlightening candle. Thank you Mom, for being there throughout my work and for all your support and blessings.

A huge bundle of thanks to all the authors and poets, who have put in their endless efforts by contributing their wonderful poems that represent the theme of this anthology. Most of the poets are much more senior than I am, and I pay my respect and honour to all of them for their full cooperation from day one of this project until the very last moment, respecting my guidelines.

A token of thanks to the poet **'Stoianka Boianova'** *from Bulgaria for writing a wonderful foreword for this anthology. Thank you for all your blessings and support. My gratitude goes out to the international poets* **'Minko Tanev'** *from Bulgaria &* **'Donna McCabe'** *from the UK for taking out their valuable time to write the previews for this anthology despite their busy schedules. Thank you both of you, your words have beautified our anthology.*

A word of thanks to all my respected teachers who always showed me the right path in my life and brimmed my heart with their blessings. A lovable token of gratitude to my brothers, sisters and all family members for their love and support always. My regards and love to all friends, far and near. Special thanks to all children of the world to whom we have dedicated this anthology. Last but not least, it will be unfair if I forget to thank the Notion Press publishers, through whom the publication of this book has become possible. Thanks to the entire team for the cooperation. Thank you, readers, fellow poets and friends, for all your love and appreciation.

Dr. Sonia Gupta
(Edito

MEET THE EDITOR

Dr. Sonia Gupta (Dera Bassi, Mohali, Punjab, India)

Dr. Sonia Gupta is a poet, writer, author, reviewer, editor and translator. She writes in English, Hindi, and Punjabi languages. By profession, she is a Dentist (MDS) with a major specialisation in Oral and Maxillofacial Pathology. She writes in vivid genres of literature like poetry, stories, essays, letters, songs and many more. She has established herself as a renowned author after getting her 28 solo books published to date, of which 11 are in English and 17 are in Hindi. Her English books are poetic collections entitled 'Spectrum of Life', 'Canvas of Life...with My Pen', 'Fountain of Inspirations', 'Meeting My Soulmate', 'Silent Verses', 'Mysterious Musings of Life', 'Agony of Life', 'Miracle of Virtues', 'Acrostic Motivations', 'There is No Darkness' and 'In the Embrace of Love'. Her first English novel is coming soon. Her Hindi books include 16 collections of poetry entitled 'Zindagi Gulzar Hai', 'Ummid Ka Diya', 'Kabhi Jalte Kabhi Bujhte Chirag', 'Kuch Ankahe Ehsas', 'Prkriti Ki Gungunahat','Ujale Tumhare Hain', 'Chhappan Pushpmalaen Kanha Ko Arpit', ' Shaym Ka He Dhyan Kar', 'Jeevan Ka Aadhar Tum', 'Bhajo Madhav, Bhajo Keshav', ' Bahut Priy Naam Govinda' "Kanha Ke Hm Sb Aabhari", "Sharan Aaye Tumhari Hum", "Nman Tumhe Hai Shri Jag Palak", " Hmari Aas Hain Madhav" & " Jai Ho Madhv Tumhari" and one collection of stories entitled 'Aadmi Bne Rehne Ka Dhong'.

*Her literary journey continues with a great endeavour. She has gone through many ups and downs in her life that have directed her vision towards suffering and she expresses that with her pen. Her writings reflect her closeness to nature, life, spirituality and humanity. For her, poetry is a God-gifted boon, and she wishes to fly high wearing the wings of poetry. She has contributed to more than 100 national and international English anthologies so far. She is a regular contributor to various national and international magazines, newspapers and journals. She has translated many poems by other poets into English, Hindi and Punjabi languages. She runs a blog about the Punjabi translations of English poems by different poets throughout the world. She is the chief-editor of two online e-zines, **"CANVAS OF THOUGHTS" & "BHAV GAGAR"** in English and Hindi languages respectively. Her first poetry book in the Punjabi will be published shortly. She is an active member of various literary and creative platforms and has won several awards in writing competitions organised by these platforms. She won a 'gold and silver medal' in a Poetic World Cup contest held by Nigeria in February and May 2018 respectively, the 'Prasanna Jenn Memorial Award 2018' by the Asian Literary Society, and '5th place in the international essay writing competition on skin complexion discrimination' organised by the Literary Society of India in March 2018. One of her essays, 'Our role and responsibilities towards nation', was selected in a national essay writing competition and is part of the book 'Youth as Nation Builders.*

She is a famous name in Hindi literature, too. She writes poems, songs, ghazals, stories, essays, letters, articles and vivid forms of Hindi compositions. Besides her seven independent Hindi books, her Hindi writings are part of several international and national anthologies, newspapers, journals and magazines. She has won many awards for her Hindi writings. Her many projects are underway.

Besides poetry, she is also fond of painting, singing, cooking, knitting, designing, stitching, embroidery teaching and reading, She has won many awards in art competitions. Many of her paintings have been placed on the cover pages of various magazines. Even she herself designed the cover pages of her two English solo books entitled "Fountain of Inspirations" and "Canvas of Life...With My Pen". She is actively contributing to literature via her literary YouTube channel, Facebook page, blog, and Instagram page.

Born and brought up in a family of well-educated people, Dr. Sonia is living her life with simplicity and a mission to do something meaningful. She considers her family her biggest inspiration, as they have always motivated her in each and every phase of her life. She feels proud to have such grandparents who have enriched their children and grandchildren with ideal virtues and morals. Her grandfather is retired from the Indian Army and serves selflessly for society till today, even at the age of 97, and believes in doing his tasks on his own. Her grandmother left this materialistic world in 2020. She was a homemaker, who not only taught her Hindi language since her birth but also made her capable of learning other skills like cooking, knitting and embroidery. Dr. Sonia lost her father, Late Sh. Devinder Kumar, in April 2019, who retired as a Government English Lecturer. He lived his entire life for his children's bright future, and it is his efforts that have led Dr. Sonia and her brothers achieve their goals. As a teacher, he was a renowned name in academics who guided a number of students who are working in well-recognized positions in society today. She is living her life following his teachings and footprints. Her mother, Mrs. Nirmal Devi, is retired as a private secretary from the Higher Education Department. Panchkula, Haryana. She is her best friend, who has always motivated and accompanied her in her every adventure, whether related to her profession, passion or personal life. Dr. Sonia feels fortunate to get two younger brothers, who have always stood beside her in even the darkest phases of her life, encouraging her to move ahead. She considers them the pillars of her life. One of her brothers works as a project manager at USA based company in Houston, Texas, USA. and the youngest one is acting as a manager in the MARTUI company, Manesar, Gurugram, Haryana. He is a professional singer and is training his 9-year-old son in classical music. She feels happy to have her bhabhi like her younger sister, who has always been her best companion. She feels blessed to have many teachers who not only taught her professional skills but also appreciated her passionate ventures and today they also clap for her achievements. As a person, she is a less talkative, simple, humble, hard-working and determined personality. She prefers to utilise every single moment in doing something meaningful rather than wasting it in gossiping. She loves to work in a disciplined and organised way. She has completed her many poetry books while travelling to her work place. She is a deep believer in God and a great devotee of Lord Krishna. She is a member of the 'Mahila Mandal Sangeet Samiti' of many temples in her region and frequently participates in various religious events where she sings religious songs composed with her own pen. Her many religious books are in the process of publication.

Dr. Sonia Gupta is a renowned name in her professional field, too. She is working as an Associate Professor in the Oral Pathology Department at a Dental College near her home town. Recently, she has earned a fellowship in Forensic Odontology under Indian Board of Forensic Odontology. She serves the community by providing dental care. She has several scientific publications in PubMed and Scopus-indexed national and international journals with first authorship, and many more are under review. She is also working on three textbooks of dentistry. She is acting as a reviewer of various medical and dental journals. She actively takes part in various conferences, workshops, community health programmes and events and has presented several research papers and posters. She is a dedicated academician with the goal of making her students excel in their subjects and in developing their multitalented skills. She is enjoying her professional as well as literary journey, which is full of passion and mission.

- **ADDRESS-** *#95/3, Adarsh Nagar, Dera Bassi, Dist: Mohali, Punjab-140507, India.*
- **MOBILE-** *6280420736*
- **FACEBOOK ID** *- 100004964983747@facebook.com*
- **FACEBOOK PAGE** *- https://www.facebook.com/sonia4840/*
- **BLOG** *- http://drsoniablogspot.blogspot.in/*
- **PUNJABI TRANSLATION BLOG** *- http://passionatepunjabijourney.blogspot.com/*
- **E MAIL** *-drsoniagupta82@gmail.com.*

LIST OF POETS

ADORE YOUR

DREAMS

(An Anthology Of Poems)
(Paperback, 1st Edition, DECEMBER 2024)

Compiled & Edited By
Dr. Sonia Gupta

follow
your
DREAMS

1. Adore Your Dreams

Dreams are nothing but guide to one's life,
Igniting a spark of inspiration, they keep us alive,
Dreams are the first step towards reality,
They make us realize our potential and capability.

Dreams are the father of new inventions,
They open locks of success to achieve ambitions,
Even in solitude, they are the best companion,
They fly in the dreamland with wings of imagination.

O' dear keep dreaming until death departs,
With their magical wand, paint a canvas,
Have courage to transform dreams into aims,
Dreams can bestow you with name and fame.

ADORE YOUR DREAMS, keep them alive always,
Let them turn into reality following proper ways,
Let them bloom like blooming flowers in a garden,
Paint them with colours of joy and passion.

© Dr. Sonia Gupta
(Editor)
*****Title Poem*****

2. Dream Big

O' you are blessed with a wonderful life,
It's a journey where one has to struggle to survive,
Accept its hurdles and move on boldly,
Leave all worries and live fearlessly.

Why be scared and afraid of anything?
Fear is a worm that engulfs every being,
Believe in your inner self and potential,
Live fearlessly; you will cherish miracles.

Dream big to turn it into reality,
Nothing is impossible actually,
Keep alive your dream always,
It will definitely bloom one day.

© Abhishek Gupta

About the Poet

Abhishek Gupta

(Gurugram, Haryana, India)
abhi.4870@gmail.com

He is not a regular poet but writes with passion in his leisure time. He writes in English, Hindi & Punjabi languages. He is also fond of music, singing, art and playing badminton, cricket and chess. Holding a degree in B-Tech (Electronics), he is working as a manager in Maruti Suzuki company at Manesar. He is also a professional singer, with his own YouTube channel. He actively participates in various creative and literary events and has received numerous awards for his skills and talents.

3. Attain Your Dreams

Two ladders astride must a human clamber,
To ensure his life he doesn't damper,
The former is for lifestyle applied,
And helps one physically tide.

The latter though is one's life's guide,
It aids one to ethics abide,
Your thoughts on both these ladders, images do create,
Of how you wish your present to your future translate.

If your wish, yet very obscure,
Transforms to a goal crystal clear,
Galloping towards the aim attains,
Your dreams so very dear.

Do envision a magical life for yourself,
And tenaciously attain your dreams,
Mould your own future continually,
And ensure your life beams.

© Ambika Gibikote Tadipatri

About the Poet

Ambika Gibikote Tadipatri

(Sydney, Australia)
ambikaprasaddoo@gmail.com

She is a poet, playwright & writer. She writes in the English language. She is associated with various literary and creative platforms. Her work has been featured in several national and international magazines, journals, newspapers and anthologies. She has received many awards for her write-ups. She is also passionate about classical dancing, drama and scriptural studies. Holding multiple degrees and certificates, currently she is working as an English educator.

4. *Hide & Seek*

O' in the veil of night
So many dreams
Play a game
Of hide and seek.

Awakening us
From our sleep
They take us
To the existence too deep.

They are pain reliever
Energy booster
Sometimes they are
Our healers.

Cherish these dreams
Until last breath
These dreams are real
Not any myth.

© Amit Kumar

About the Poet

Amit Kumar

(Ambala Cantt, Haryana, India)
Amit123@gmail.com

He is a 11-year-old budding poet studying in 6th grade. He writes in English & Hindi languages. He is also fond of reading, art and singing. He actively participates in various creative events organized by her school and other organizations. He has received many prizes for her creativity. He is passionate for literature.

5. Not for Dream Sake

In my eyes
I cherish
So many dreams…

But not only
For dreams sake…

But for
Turning them
Into
My ambition
One day…

© *Anna Ferriero*

About the Poet

Anna Ferriero
(Torre del Greco, Italy)
annaferriero71@yahoo.it

She is a bilingual poet, writer & translator. She writes in English & Italian languages. She is associated with various literary and creative platforms. Her work has been featured in several national and international magazines, journals, newspapers and anthologies. She has received many awards for her write-ups. She has translated many poems throughout the world into Italian language. She is a representative of Italy in India at Güncel Sanat Dergisi. Currently, she is a student, university researcher and doctor of honoris causa.

6. Dreaming

Life is a journey,
A journey that ends one day,
Day will end,
End not the dreams.

Dreams are our hopes,
Hopes for tomorrow,
Tomorrow becomes better,
Better if we dream today.

Today whatever you are dreaming,
Dreaming may become living,
Living with this inspiration,
Inspiration comes for the future.

© Dr. Annie Evangelin. N

About the Poet

Dr. Annie Evangelin. N
(Vellore, Tamilnadu, India)
ann18eva@gmail.com

She is not a regular writer but writes with passion in her leisure time. She has contributed to many literary activities during her academic and professional career. By profession, she is a Dentist with a major specialty in Oral and Maxillofacial Surgery. She has received many accolades in her academics and profession.

7. Give You I Will

Give me just a
Drop of your distress
Give you I will
Distinctive a cup of adventure.

Give me just a
Bit of your bad memory
Give you I will
Elegant a dream's elevator.

Give me just a
Moment of your life
Give you I will
My entire life.

© Atmaja Mishra

About the Poet

Atmaja Mishra
(Kashinagar, Odisha, India)
prasantmisra87@gmail.com

She is a differently abled budding poet and writer. She writes in the English & Odia languages. She is also fond of art, reading, tattoo designing and music. She actively participates in various creative events organized by different organizations. She has attained multiple certifications in hands. She has a deep interest in literature and wishes to fly high wearing the wings of poetry. Currently, she is in wheelchair, struggling with her disability but she has not left her passion for poetry.

8. Credit Yourself

The path you follow,
Never be hollow,
The service you render,
Forever there to glow.

Nights become slow,
Dreams to flow,
Thoughts be positive,
Mission be progressive.

If vision is affirmative,
Ideas taken constrictive,
Nothing be destructive,
All is within you.

Stored in plenty too,
Why not credit you?
All that you are absolutely true,
Keep dreaming to turn them true.

© Ayushi Pradhani

About the Poet

Ayushi Pradhani
(Balangir, Odisha, India)
pradhaniramesh212@gmail.com

She is a 14-year-old budding poet studying in 9th grade. She writes in the English language. She is also fond of reading, art, dancing and singing. She actively participates in various creative events organized by her school. She has received many prizes for her creativity. She wishes to fly high spreading the wings of poetry.

9. Even When I Fail

Even when I fail, I never lose hope till the end,
I keep dreaming, beyond any extent,
Life has two sides; positive and negative,
Can never exist without being cooperative.

Life is not what you think or I,
As your wrong may be right for me,
And your right be wrong for others,
Life is beautiful, and we strive not to make it defile.

Dare to dream big and fulfil it,
Whatever may be the situation, don't leave it,
There definitely comes one day,
When your dreams fruitfully turn into reality.

© Ayushman Pradhani

About the Poet

Ayushman Pradhani
(Balangir, Odisha, India)
pradhaniramesh212@gmail.com

He is an 11-year-old budding poet studying in 8th grade. He writes in the English language. He is also fond of reading, art and music. He actively participates in various creative events organized by his school and other organizations. He has received many prizes for his creativity. He wishes to fly high spreading the wings of poetry.

10. Visionaries Dream

New York to Shanghai
In 40 minutes
Can anyone think of it?
Only Elon Musk can do it
With SpaceX's plan.

APJ Abdul Kalam
Had a dream to see
India to be a Developed Country by 2020
How many could have thought of?

Students have dreams of
Leaders, Scientists, Reformers
Which they say often
Can those dreams be possible
Without perseverance but remain in procrastination?

©Damodar Boruah

About the Poet

Damodar Boruah
(Kakodonga, Assam, India)
damodarboruah14@gmail.com

He is a bilingual poet, writer, author & translator. He writes in Assamese & English languages. He is associated with various literary and creative platforms. His work has been featured in several national and international magazines, journals, newspapers and anthologies. He has received many awards for his write-ups. Holding multiple degrees, currently, he is working as a farmer and Coacher for aspiring students to appear Sainik School and Jawahar Navodaya Vidyalaya Entrance Examinations.

11. Incomplete Story

In life, it is normal for all of us
To have dreams
Dreams could be good or bad
There is always a story.

How do we take our dreams,
It depends on us,
We do dream of our departed loved ones,
And it tells us a story.

Story of their incomplete tasks,
Which we must do for them,
Sometimes these tasks are difficult to achieve
But we know they will guide us.

Some dreams are meant to remind us
Of what we have done good or bad
No matter what
We must always try to remember our dreams.

© David Soh

About the Poet

David Soh

(Singapore)
davidsoh.books@gmail.com

He is a poet, writer & author. He writes in the English language. He has authored two independent poetry books. He is associated with various literary and creative platforms. His work has been featured in several national and international magazines, journals, newspapers and anthologies. He has received many awards for his write-ups. He is a high school graduate and currently working as a Financial Adviser Representative.

12. I Will Wait

Love, peace and humanity,
No racism and inequality,
Are my only dreams,
Which I want to cherish in reality.

May be today, in the modern era,
Era of corruption and inhumanity,
These dreams can't be fulfilled,
Can't be cherished.

But I am sure about it,
One day they will come true,
I will wait for it,
I will adore my dreams to infinite.

© Fady Bouaz

About the Poet

Fady Bouaz

(Lebanon, Arab)
boazfady@gmail.com

He is a bilingual poet & writer. He writes in English & Arabian languages. He is associated with various literary and creative platforms. His work has been featured in several national and international magazines, journals, newspapers and anthologies. He has received many awards for his write-ups. Currently, he works as a carpenter and freelance writer.

13. Middlemen's Dream

When price will decrease?
More will be purchased ,
And can give essentials,
To children what they ask.

EMIs, multiple EMIs,
For resolving multiple problems,
Gradually going deeper and deeper,
And dream when to recover from (it).

Little could do to be Free,
What can't they do in life,
Try their children to fulfill their own dream,
Will children become misusing their time?

© Glory Shikha Boruah

About the Poet

Glory Shikha Boruah
(Kakodonga, Assam, India)
damodarboruah14@gmail.com

She is a 17-year-old budding poet studying in 11th grade. She writes in the English language. She is also fond of reading, painting, dancing and singing. She actively participates in various creative events organized by her school She has received many prizes for her creativity. She got the inspiration of writing from his own father "Damodar Boruah" who is a poet. She wishes to fly high spreading the wings of poetry.

14. I Will Not Succumb

Though the odds are stacked irrevocably against solitary me,
I vow to never succumb nor give in nor give up,
For those facing tyranny and not expressing it,
Are equivalent of emptying God's ever replenishing cup.

I will fight back for I am in the pangs of hurtful pain,
Trying my utmost to grasp for air and not succumb,
For I am indeed made of stronger and sterner stuff,
willing to sweat it out until my bones are numb.

Indeed, life is not fair when the means are foul,
To uproot an innocent soul who will falter and fall,
So, I should courageously spring forth,
And stand proud, resolute and tall.

I have dreams in my eyes to fulfil them,
And I am sure to accomplish them,
Even if life takes me to the toughest pathway,
I am sure, my dreams will come true one day.

© Heera Nawaz

About the Poet

Heera Nawaz
(Bengaluru, Karnataka, India)
nawazheera@gmail.com

She is a poet & writer. She writes in the English language. She is associated with various literary and creative platforms. Her work has been featured in several national and international magazines, journals, newspapers and anthologies. She has received many awards for her write-ups. Holding an M.A. (English), currently, she is working as an educator and freelance writer.

15. I'll Fly Like a Bird

Like a bird on joyful wing,
My feet just fly, my heart doth sing,
I'm O, so free to just be me,
As high as the sky, as blue as the sea.

I float with glee, I twirl on my toes,
Like bird's wings flutter, as the wild wind blows,
Sweet freedom I feel, like the winsome breeze,
My feelings just soar, like heat, by degrees.

I'm free to dream, by my heart's desire,
My feelings float, like a billowing fire,
High above the world, my dream doth grow,
I skim the clouds, I skip to and fro.

I swoop down low, my arms fling high,
My feet dance lightly, as I heave a sigh,
There are no fetters to hold me down,
Without any tethers, my dream wears a crown.

© Kathy Jo Blake-Bryant

About the Poet

Kathy Jo Blake-Bryant
(Bates City, Missouri, USA)
kathyjopoetree@gmail.com

She is a poet, writer & author. She writes in the English language. She has authored four independent poetry books. She is associated with various literary and creative platforms. Her work has been featured in several national and international magazines, journals, newspapers and anthologies. She has received many awards for her write-ups. She is a high school graduate and currently, working as a Domestic Engineer and enjoying her passion of poetry.

16. Remember

Forget the world,
Forget the universe,
Forget the people,
Forget the achievements.

But remember…
Always one thing,
Today and forever,
Within your heart and mind.

Never ever forget
To dream
And to
Cherish their existence.

© Dr. Kinza Qureshi

About the Poet

Dr. Kinza Qureshi

(New York, USA)
kinza309@gmail.com

She is not a regular writer but writes with passion in her leisure time. She has contributed to many literary activities during her academic and professional career. By profession, she is a Dentist with a major speciality in Prosthodontics. She has received many accolades in her academics and profession. She is also fond of reading, listening to music and photography.

17. I Believe

My dreams
May be small
Or ordinary.

But for me
They are big
And special.

And I believe
In my
Dreams.

One day
They will bring
Miracles.

© Lynsey McCabe

About the Poet

Lynsey McCabe
(Rhondda, South Wales, UK)
donna_salisbury@sky.com

She is a 14-year-old budding poet studying in the second year of comprehensive school. She writes in the English language. She is also fond of reading, art and music. She actively participates in various literary and creative events organized by her school and other organizations. She has received many prizes for her artwork and poetry. She got the inspiration for writing from her own mother, 'Donna McCabe'. She wishes to touch the heights of poetry.

18. Yet I Live

Since my birth
My eyes
Cherished
So many dreams.

Some fulfilled
Some remained incomplete
Yet I love
All of them.

Incomplete dreams
Will definitely
Be fulfilled
One day, I am sure.

© Manmohan Rohilla

About the Poet

Manhoman Rohilla
(Gurugram, Haryana, India)
rohillasahab9050@gmail.com

He is a 21-year-old budding poet studying in his final year, at Government Polytechnic. He is passionate about poetry and music. He writes in English & Hindi languages. He actively participates in various literary and creative events organized by his institute and other organizations. He has received many awards for his creativity. He wishes to go for a mile in the field of literature.

19. Chain of Dreams

Life is to live
To its fullest
Keep dreaming
And put efforts
To give your best.

Weave the chain
Of endless dreams
Let this chain
Never be broken
Until you live.

© *Meena Panchal*

About the Poet

Meena Panchal

(Faridabad, Haryana, India)
meenapanchl224@gmail.com

She is a 20-year-old budding poet studying in final year at Government Polytechnic, Faridabad. She is passionate about poetry and fashion designing. She writes in English & Hindi languages. She actively participates in various literary and creative events organized by her institute and other organizations. She has received many awards for her creativity. She wishes to go a mile in the field of literature along with her passion for fashion designing and art.

20. I Wish

I may be
A little girl
My eyes
May be tiny.

But my dreams
Are big
And vast
Beyond limits.

I wish to
Fulfil
Them all
Without any second thought.

© Meher Mathur

About the Poet

Meher Mathur

(Pune, Maharashtra, India)
kshtjpandey879@gmail.com

She is a 6-year-old budding poet studying in 1ˢᵗ grade. She writes in the English & Hindi languages. She is also fond of drawing. She actively participates in various literary and creative events organized by her school and other organizations. She has received many prizes for her creativity. She wishes to fly high spreading the wings of poetry.

21. Whatsoever They Are

Live life
With a determination
Whatever
May be the situation.

Dare to dream big
And meaningful
And achieve them
You will feel wonderful.

Dreams make us
Dreams break us
Whatsoever they are
They don't leave us.

© Muskan Vashisth

About the Poet

Muskan Vashisth
(Faridabad, Haryana, India)
muskanvashisht184@gmail.com

She is a 20-year-old budding poet studying in her final year at Government Polytechnic, Faridabad. She writes in English & Hindi languages. She is passionate about fashion designing and music. She actively participates in various literary and creative events organized by her institute and other organizations. She has received many awards for her creativity.

22. I Simply Dream

Some dream about
Being rich
Some dream about
Being healthy.

Some dream about
Being famous
Some dream about
Being boss.

But I simply
Dream about
Being a
Good human being.

© Namrata Dubey

About the Poet

Namrata Dubey
(Faridabad, Haryana, India)
nd7578509@gmail.com

She is a 23-year-old budding poet studying in her final year, data basement management. She is passionate about poetry and reading books. She writes in English & Hindi languages. She actively participates in various literary and creative events organized by her institute and other organizations. She has received many awards for her creativity. She wishes to spread positivity through her poetry.

23. O' My Dreams

O my dreams
Come !
Come to my eyes.

I yearn to
Behold you
Within me.

I wish to
Make you
Forever truth.

© Nibir Neerlov Borah

About the Poet

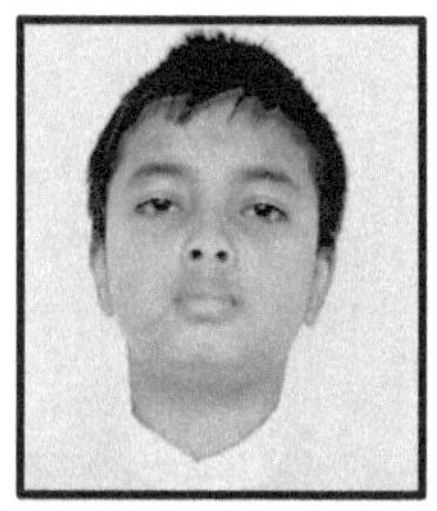

Nibir Neerlov Borah

(Titabor, Assam, India)
damodarboruah14@gmail.com

He is a 12-year-old budding poet studying in 6th grade. He writes in the English language. He is also fond of playing guitar. He actively participates in various literary and creative events organized by his school and other organizations. He has received many prizes for his creativity. He wishes to fly high spreading the wings of poetry.

24. Make Them Shine

We get this life once,
Why waste in violence?
Set your dreams
And ambitions.

Take steps to
Follow them
Put efforts to
Adore them.

Don't let these dreams
To be dreams
Have courage to
Make them shine like sunbeams.

© Nirmal Devi

About the Poet

Nirmal Devi
(Mohali, Punjab, India)
nirmaldevi@gmail.com

She is not a regular poet but writes with passion. She writes in English, Hindi and Punjabi languages. She is also fond of art, singing, cooking, dancing and knitting. Retired as a personal secretary from Haryana Education Dept. Panchkula, currently, she works as a housewife and social worker.

25. My Papa's Dream

To fulfil
My papa's dream
Is my only
Dream…

To become
A singer
A superstar
And a good human being…

O' my Lord!
Bless me always
To fulfil
My dream…

© Nishant Gupta

About the Poet

Nishant Gupta
(Gurugram, Haryana, India)
abhi.4870@gmail.com

He is a 10 -year-old budding poet studying in 6th grade. He is passionate about poetry, music and art. He writes in English & Hindi languages. He is also a singer and getting training in classical music. He is fond of swimming, skating, playing badminton, cricket and chess. He actively participates in various literary and creative events organized by his school and other organizations. He has received many awards for his creativity. Recently, he performed as a singer in one of the renowned entertainment shows 'Junior Superstar Season-3' on Sony TV. He wishes to fly high spreading the wings of poetry and music.

26. Embrace of Dreams

Live in the embrace
Of your
Dreams…

Dreams are
Your best
Companions…

They will lead you
Further
In your life…

Keep holding
Their hands
To cherish your life.

© Nishu Kushavaha

About the Poet

Nishu Kushavaha

(Faridabad, Haryana, India)
nishukmri2006@gmail.com

She is an 18-year-old budding poet studying in her 2nd year at Government Polytechnic, Faridabad. She is passionate about poetry and fashion designing. She writes in English & Hindi languages. She actively participates in various literary and creative events organized by her institute and other organizations. She has received many awards for her creativity. She wishes to bring a positive change in the world through her pen and art.

27. You Are My Dreams

You love me endlessly,
That I do know,
For your spontaneous love,
My head I bow.

You are my heart's queen,
All the world knows,
To see your loving heart,
My hope here rose.

You are my dreams,
And you are my heart,
Nights after nights,
I many poems wrote.

I am in each word,
And in each line,
I am in all stanzas,
To turn your love fine.

© Dr. Okram Shakuntala

About the Poet

Dr. Okram Shakuntala

(Imphal, Manipur, India)
shakuntala.okram@gmail.com

She is a poet & writer. She writes in the English language. She is associated with various literary and creative platforms. Her work has been featured in several national and international magazines, journals, newspapers and anthologies. She has received many awards for her write-ups. Holding a Master in Arts and PhD, currently she works as an Asst. Prof of Economics and HOD, in The Maharaja Bodh Chandra College, Imphal.

28. Unfulfilled Dreams

Midnight
Motionless pendulums
A tick...
Unique a tick of the clock
And no more 2024
It's 25 now
Family friends
Celebrations...
Reflections lookbacks
Lookaheads ....
Yes, we can do
We can be...
Be what we exactly wish...
Imperative a strategy
A strategy again for survival ...
And all unfulfilled dreams…
Are about to be fulfilled soon!

© Prasant Misra

About the Poet

Prasant Misra
(Kashinagar, Odisha, India)
prasantmisra87@gmail.com

He is a bilingual poet & writer. He writes in English & Odia languages. He has authored four Odia and one English poetic collection. He is associated with various literary and creative platforms. His work has been featured in several national and international magazines, journals, newspapers and anthologies. He has received many awards for his write-ups. Holding an M.A. (Odia language and literature), currently, he is working as a journalist.

29. A Big World

In the small world
Of mine
A big world
Exists.

A world
Full of
My dreams
And wishes.

Every moment
I cherish
This world
As my original world.

© Radhika Rohilla

About the Poet

Radhika Rohilla
(Gurugram, Haryana, India)
radhikarohilla9050@gmail.com

She is a 17-year-old budding poet studying in her 2nd year at government Polytechnic. She is passionate about poetry and fashion designing. She writes in English & Hindi languages. She actively participates in various literary and creative events organized by her institute and other organizations. She has received many awards for her creativity. She wishes to go a mile in the field of literature along with her passion for fashion designing and art.

30. Live Each Moment

Life is a pathway
To cherish each day
God has blessed us
With this gift.

Let each day
Be filled with
Fruitful dreams
And ambitions.

Live each moment
With dreams so high
Positive
And meaningful.

© Ramanivas Tiwari

About the Poet

Ramanivas Tiwari
(Sitapur, Uttar Pradesh, India)
ramanivas40@gmail.com

He is a bilingual poet and writer. He writes mostly in Hindi and less frequently in the English language. He is associated with various literary and creative platforms. His work has been featured in several national and international magazines, journals, newspapers and anthologies. He has received many awards for his Hindi write-ups. This is his first English anthology. Holding an M.A. (Hindi), he retired as a teacher and currently, works as a freelance writer and a social worker.

31. What You Want

Blame not yourself for being victimized,
Let's take time to surmise,
See things positive to humanize,
Yourself with others to rise,
Up to the mark you ever realize.

Better to love those who hate you,
Detest them who love you,
With time,
Everyone comes to your line,
Never think of I, me and mine.

Do what you love to do,
Dream what you want to do,
Changes will come to see,
If you change yourself in glee,
Negativity sure to away flee.

© Ramesh Chandra Pradhani

About the Poet

Ramesh Chandra Pradhani

(Balangir, Odisha, India)
pradhaniramesh212@gmail.com

He is a trilingual poet & writer. He writes in English, Hindi & Odia languages. He has authored six solo books. He is associated with various literary and creative platforms. His work has been featured in several national and international magazines, journals, newspapers and anthologies. He has received many awards for his write-ups. Holding multiple degrees, currently, he is working as a Principal at P S Degree Mahavidyalaya Deogaon, Odisha.

32. I Will Keep Fighting

Progression and regression
Victory and defeat
Are part of life
Why should I be afraid of these?

Rather than being afraid
Why should not I fight with them?
Why should not I move with determination?
And keep my dream alive.

The one who is afraid of hurdles
He or she is known as a coward
Without any identity
He or she lives in this world.

Why should I be called a coward?
Why should I lose my identity,
Rather than that
I will keep fighting to keep my dream alive.

© Remy Pandey

About the Poet

Remy Pandey
(Bengaluru, Karnataka, India)
kshtjpandey879@gmail.com

She is a bilingual poet & writer. She writes in Hindi & English languages. She is associated with various literary and creative platforms. Her Hindi work has been featured in several international and national magazines, journals, anthologies and newspapers. She has won many awards for her write-ups. This is her first English anthology. She has a B. A philosophy Honours. Currently, she works as homemaker and freelance writer.

33. My Determination

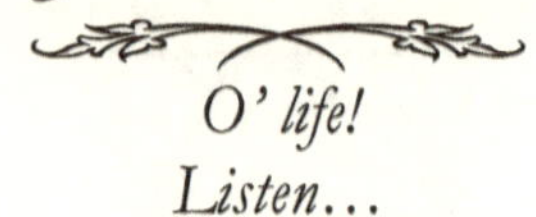

You may bring
So many downs
And hurdles…

But I am
Determined
Very much

To turn my
Every dream
Into a reality.

© **Ritika Kumari**

About the Poet

Ritika Kumari
(Ambala Cantt, Haryana, India)
Ritika44@gmail.com

Shi is an 11-year-old budding poet studying in 6th grade. She writes in English & Hindi languages. She is also fond of reading, art and singing. She actively participates in various creative events organized by her school and other organizations. She has received many prizes for her creativity.

34. Butterfly

A Butterfly
Flies
Spreading its
Wings…

Comes to my
Dreamland
Bringing
Joy and smile…

I love
Her very much
As my
Best buddy.

© **Rivyansh Rohilla**

About the Poet

Rivyansh Rohilla

(Dehradun Uttarakhand, India
Rivyansh0312rohilla@gmail.com

Hi is a 12-year-old budding poet studying in 7 grade. He writes in English & Hindi languages. He is also fond of reading, art and football playing. He actively participates in various creative events organized by his school and other organizations. He has received many prizes for his creativity.

35. I Adore You

Dreams! Dreams! Dreams!
Who are you?

From where do you come?
To where do you go?

I could not understand
Your mystery.

But still
I adore you.

And I
Always yearn for you.

© Saanvi Gupta

About the Poet

Saanvi Gupta
(Gurugram, Haryana, India)
abhi.4870@gmail.com

She is a 7-year-old budding poet studying in 2nd class. She writes in English and Hindi languages. She is also fond of singing, playing badminton, skating and painting. She actively participates in various cultural events in her school and has received many prizes.

36. To Reach a World

I am a little
Doll
I wish to
Fly high
With
The wings
Of my dreams
To reach
A world
Filled with
New hopes
And wishes.

© *Sanchi Kumari*

About the Poet

Sanchi Kumari

(Dera Bassi, Punjab, India)
<u>Sunny128@gmail.com</u>

She is a 6-year-old budding poet studying in 1st class. She writes in English and Hindi languages. She is also fond of singing, playing and painting. She actively participates in various cultural events in her school and has received many prizes.

37. Fly, Fly

Fly, fly Oh my dreams,
The way I dream of you,
Fly like a free bird,
Into a world without limits.

Fly, fly Oh my dreams,
Free and bold,
To unprecedented heights,
To fulfil my heart's desire.

Fly, fly Oh my dreams,
Spread wishes under the sky,
Fly all over the universe,
Bring peace and freedom to everyone.

© Seadeta Bela Juric

About the Poet

Seadeta Bela Juric

(Bosnia and Herzegovina)
Seadetajurić@gmail. Com

She is a bilingual poet & writer. She writes in English & Bosnian languages. She is associated with various literary and creative platforms. Her work has been featured in several national and international magazines, journals, newspapers and anthologies. She has received many awards for her write-ups. Retired as a teacher, she is living as a housewife.

38. Dream More

Life is a struggle,
Every moment a new hurdle,
But don't leave hope,
And determination.

Keep dreaming,
And dream more,
Cherish them,
And adore.

Dreams will take you,
To another world,
Full of,
New hopes.

© Shamsher Singh Rohilla

About the Poet

Shamsher Singh Rohilla

(Gurugram, Haryana, India)

shamshers44@gmail.com

❧❧❧

He is a bilingual poet & writer. He writes in English & Hindi languages. He is associated with various literary and creative platforms. His work has been featured in several national and international magazines, journals, newspapers and anthologies. He has received many awards for his write-ups. Holding a B.A., currently he works as a Quality Officer in a private company.

❧❧❧

39. Me and My Dreamland

Me and my dreamland
Both are special
Weaving special
Dreams.

Dreams that none else
Might have seen
And I dare
To see such dreams.

I pray
To Almighty
To give me strength
Of fulfilling my dreams.

© **Sheetal Kumari**

About the Poet

Sheetal Kumari
(Faridabad, Haryana, India)
skumari06092007@gmail.com

She is a 17-year-old budding poet studying in her 2nd year of diploma in data base management at Government Polytechnic, Faridabad. She writes in English & Hindi languages. She is also passionate about fashion designing & music. She actively participates in various literary and creative events organized by her institute and other organizations. She has received many awards for her creativity.

40. Even in My Dreams

I loved and I lost
To a young man, my heart,
Oh so handsome, I thought,
I was bewitched and besot.

He paid me no heed,
He seemed not to need,
Me or my love indeed,
I could feel my heart bleed.

Then fate threw us apart,
The heartbreak soon forgot,
Immersed in my work,
Day and night would I slog.

I was now mature and kind,
In appearance and in my mind,
My true love who complimented me like hand and glove,
This love, I knew would never be lost.

Even in my dreams, I cherish this love.
It is indeed a gift from above.

© Dr. Shyamala Annavarapu

About the Poet

Dr. Shyamala Annavarapu
(Hyderabad, Telangana, India)
shyamala.annavarapu@gmail.com

She is a poet, writer & doctor. She writes in the English language. She is associated with various literary and creative platforms. Her work has been featured in several national and international magazines, journals, newspapers and anthologies. She has received many awards in academic as well as literature. She is a postgraduate in gynaecology and currently, working as a private practitioner.

41. Day Dreams

Dreams are of different kinds
Some of the dreams live with us
But, some dreams disappear
As if they are the shadows of the vision.

They give us wishes and wills
As compliments but leave us
Not available when it is required
To remain with.

We may be compelled
To stay asleep
As it helped us to be lazy
There is no question.

Where to go
From where to come
The perennial question is that
One and only that.

© Sreedharan Parokode

About the Poet

Sreedharan Parokode
(Kozhikode, Kerala, India)
sreeparokode@gmail.com

He is a bilingual poet, writer, author & lyricist. He writes in English & Malayalam languages. He has 30 solo poetry books to his credit. He is associated with various literary and creative platforms. His work has been featured in several national and international magazines, journals, newspapers and anthologies. He has received many awards for his write-ups. Holding multiple degrees, he is retired from Calicut University. Currently, he is enjoying his literary journey.

42. *Have Courage*

Who says
We dream
Only at night?

Daring minds
Dream
Even while awaken.

Have courage
To see dreams
Even when awaken.

And dare to turn
Them into
Reality.

Steven McCabe

About the Poet

Steven McCabe

(Rhondda, South Wales, UK)
donna_salisbury@sky.com

He is not a regular poet but writes with passion. He writes in the English language. He is also fond of music, traveling, playing football, going gym and having cars. He actively participates in various creative and literary events. He has served in the army for 4 years before leaving and getting married. Currently, he works full-time and takes care of his family.

43. Reflections of Dark

Slumbering eyes visualise
Flashing images of known and unknown
Like a cinema screening tragedies
Good fortunes arrives
Pertaining to self
No one intrudes
A companion by your side
Until your final day
Some disturbances interrupt your sleep
We scream, thinking it's real
Good memories linger
In-depth visualisation of subconscious mind
Our dear ones who left us in tears
Visit us in dreams
Magical concoction of sleep
Sweet, bitter lasts long..

© Sulochana Narayanan

About the Poet

Sulochana Narayanan
(Palakkad, Kerala, India)
sulsubra@gmail.com

She is a bilingual poet & writer She writes in English & Tamil languages. She has published a solo English poetry book "Imprints". She is associated with various literary and creative platforms. Her work has been featured in several national and international magazines, journals, newspapers and anthologies. She has received many awards for her write-ups. She is also fond of paintings, music and reading. Holding an M.A. (English) and B.Ed., currently, she works as an academician.

44. Their Dreams

I see
My parents
Living every moment…

With dreams
In their eyes
For us…

And they sacrificed
Their own dreams
For us.

I always wish
To respect
Such parents and their dreams.

© Sunny Kumar

About the Poet

Sunny Kumar
(Dera Bassi, Punjab, India)
Sunny148@gmail.com

He is a 16 -year-old budding poet studying in 11th standard. He is passionate about poetry and music. He writes in English & Hindi languages. He actively participates in various literary and creative events organized by his institute and other organizations. He has received many awards for his creativity. He wishes to go for a mile in the field of literature.

45. Keep True

The gracefulness of a youthful time,
How glorious is the youth life-line,
Where hope and poesy entwine,
Youth is the season of dream to win.

Keep true to the dreams of youth,
Act as what you do makes the truth,
Never dull your shine on your dream;
Hope of today is tomorrow's joy of stream.

Remember your hasting days fly fast,
Unfurl your victory flag atop the mast,
Set your rudder today, there's no tomorrow,
In youth, Success is yours; there's no sorrow.

© Surendra Singnar

About the Poet

Surendra Singnar
(Diphu, Assam, India)
Singnar.s@gmail.com

He is a bilingual poet & writer. He writes in English & Assamese languages. He has authored 2 solo poetry books. He is associated with various literary and creative platforms. His work has been featured in several national and international magazines, journals, newspapers and anthologies. He has received many awards for his write-ups. Retired as a high school teacher, currently, he works as a social worker.

46. Dreams That Awaken

In the soft shadow of the night,
where the soul dares to fly,
dreams are born without reproach,
with light that begins to shine.

They are rivers of living hope,
that fill the heart with joy,
they are intense and noble forces
inviting us to walk new goals.

Dreams that paint golden paths,
and take us far from fear,
drawing a future I implore,
a horizon without pain.

Each dream is a step forward,
an impulse of faith and joy,
life becomes radiant,
when a dream guides each day.

© Taghrid Bou Merhi

About the Poet

Taghrid Bou Merhi

(Foz Do Iguaçu, Paraná, Brasil)
taghrid240@gmail.com

She is a multilingual poet, writer, editor, translator and journalist. She has authored 17 books and translated 24 books to date. She is associated with various literary and creative platforms. Her work has been featured in several national and international magazines, journals, newspapers and anthologies. She has received many awards for her write-ups. Currently, she is working as an Arabic language teacher for non-native speakers.

47. Lead to the Truth

He never seems to have a dream in his eyes
One can be so indifferent, I can't even realise.

When there are clouds in the sky,
The rain in his eyes seems to satisfy,
The sun is absorbed by his chirping hand,
By their best way,
All truths are grasped without end.

He said, the idol is never be the truth,
We are in the same tree,
We are our own flower and fruit,
I saw him from the rise in all the mission,
Firmly the same no matter what's the occasion,
Nobody able to take his mind in the right place,
And it always seems that he is truly dreamless !

Today I think, we failed with our polish brute.
Crying in a dream can easily lead to the truth.

© Tapas Mahapatra

About the Poet

Tapas Mahapatra
Kolkata, West Bengal, India,
tapasmahapatra025@gmail.com

He is a bilingual poet, writer, author & translator. He writes in Bengali & English languages. He has authored 8 solo Bengali Poetry books. He is associated with various literary and creative platforms. His work has been featured in several national and international magazines, journals, newspapers and anthologies. He has received many awards for his write-ups. He is a Graduate of Calcutta University and currently works as a journalist.

48. Finding You

You and me
Got tied in a knot
Of love and faith.

It was a prolonged
Dream of mine
To find you.

And today....
Destiny became
Blissful.

Finding you in reality
I feel …
Totally wonderful.

© Dr. Vaishnavi S

About the Poet

Dr. Vaishnavi S
(Hyderabad, Telangana, India)
vaishnavisecenec@gmail.com

She is not a regular writer but writes with passion in her leisure time. She has contributed to many literary activities during her academic and professional career. By profession, she is a Dentist with major speciality in Oral and Maxillofacial Pathology. She has received many accolades in her academics and profession. She is also fond of travelling and listening to music.

49. My Dream, My Identity

I am a Doctor..
Such a noble profession,
Selflessly serving,
People of my nation.

From the core of my heart,
I pay gratitude,
To the great Almighty!
For honouring me with such honour.

My dream today,
Has become my identity,
O' Lord!
I am thankful to you for that deeply.

© Dr. Vidhya Selvaraj

About the Poet

Dr. Vidhya Selvaraj

(Chennai, Tamilnadu, India)
dr.rsvidhya@gmail.com

She is not a regular writer but writes with passion in her leisure time. She has contributed to many literary activities during her academic and professional career. By profession, she is a Dentist with major speciality in Orthodontics. She has received many accolades in her academics and profession. She is also fond of travelling, cooking and photography.

50. Choice Is Yours

O' dear this life is yours; it depends on how you live,
Efforts are yours; it depends on how much you give,
Situations will come to break you down,
Choice is yours whether you stay strong or mourn.

At every step, you will be encompassed by challenges,
Every day will bring unexpected changes,
Sometimes hope, sometimes hopelessness,
Choice is yours whether you smile or take the stress.

Loss and gain are two wheels of this life,
You have to move on further till you survive,
Besides successful glory you will face so many failures,
choice is yours whether you get disheartened or move without fear.

Keep dreaming of whatever you desire,
None can stop you here and there,
Dreams may be dreams or may become reality,
The choice is yours how you take them actually.

© Vikas Gupta

About the Poet

Vikas Gupta
(Mississauga, Ontario, Canada)
Vikas.48@gmail.com

He is not a regular poet but writes with passion. Holding degrees in B-Tech and MBA, he is working as a project manager in one of the multinational companies in the USA. He writes in English, Hindi and Punjabi languages. He is also fond of music, art, cooking, reading, traveling, and photography. He actively participates in various creative and literary events.

51. Day Will Come

Life may be tough,
Life may be rough,
There may be prickles,
There may be hurdles.

Life may try to break me,
Anywhere it can take me,
Beyond this world,
Away from my beloveds.

Yet I will keep dreaming,
I will never stop moving,
I am sure that day will come,
When my dreams will turn into my mission.

© Dr. Vinod Kumar Gupta

About the Poet

Dr. Vinod Kumar Gupta

(Noida, Uttar Pradesh, India)
atalmoradabadi@gmail.com

He is a bilingual poet & writer. He writes in English & Hindi languages. He is associated with various literary and creative platforms. His work has been featured in several national and international magazines, journals, newspapers and anthologies. He has received many awards for his write-ups. His first solo Hindi book is coming soon. Holding multiple degrees, he retired as an Engineer and currently, works as a freelance writer & social worker.

Edited & Published Anthologies from January 2023 to November 2024

Every
thing
STARTS
WITH
A
DREAM

"DREAMS ARE NOTHING BUT GUIDES TO OUR FUTURE. LIVE YOUR DREAMS, ADORE THEM AND KEEP THEM ALIVE ALWAYS UNTIL THEY COME TRUE."

DR. SONIA GUPTA

believe in your dreams

ADORE YOUR
DREAMS

(An Anthology Of Poems)
(Paperback, 1st Edition, DECEMBER 2024)

Compiled & Edited By
Dr. Sonia Gupta